Ain't Afraid to Say It

by Roosevelt & Miesha Franklin

DORRANCE
PUBLISHING CO
EST 1920
PITTSBURGH, PENNSYLVANIA 15238

Dorrance Publishing Co
585 Alpha Drive
Pittsburgh, PA 15238
Visit our website at *www.dorrancebookstore.com*

ISBN: 979-8-89127-708-3
eISBN: 979-8-89127-205-7

Every word uttered through God's Holy Spirit is truly an honor. It is our belief that all souls have been stained. The joy and hope we have in God should provide us with confidence that the stains are not permanent. The blood of his only begotten Son has the cleansing power to remove all stains, whether lightly or heavily soiled. If you're lost and wandering in the wilderness; trying to find your way; born again or rededicating your life to Christ; we pray the Holy Spirit will remind you that there is no sin greater than his saving power.

Roosevelt and Miesha

Something I Wanted to Share by Miesha Franklin

To witness God's anointed, pregnant with his words, vulnerable, obedient, transparent, and honest, has been a journey that I've been blessed to be a part of. Late nights, early mornings, drop everything and write on sight! Collaborating, tweaking, and making sure that the words were just right; not right in the way that it flows, but rather writing the words that HE chose. You see, this was assigned during a time of great adversity, and my husband, Mr. Roosevelt Franklin and I were the the vessels chosen to write not mere words, but words that revealed God's prophesying power. At times, I was chastised, other times offended, saying, "This is all about me, God has got to be kidding." I finally realized it wasn't about me, but for someone, somewhere, who reads this, it could be their saving grace. Perhaps they see themselves through something that is written, or a revelation uncovers some things in them that has been hidden. It happened to me, specifically through "Wake Up," which served as a gentle reminder—well, maybe just a reminder that as a Christian, we should strive to let our lights shine. We shouldn't have to walk around wearing masks. We should live our lives how we actually want to be seen. Besides, is your mask really covering everything, or does it have you on display under brightest lights from the One who actually matters? "Wake Up" is humbler, simply put. I saw myself again in the "Ugly Truth"; the flesh is powerful if you don't have enough of the Holy Spirit to suppress it. "The Ugly Truth" made me feel so ugly that I began to jot down bits and pieces of my own testimony. It sparked something that I've included in this God-assigned publishing which I'm blessed to have participated; knowingly or unknowingly contributing by my actions, thoughts, or words. To my husband, thank you for being a fearless leader. I've seen your struggles. I've seen your pain. I've watched you get chastised, beat down, and get up with the strength to stand flat-footed with Satan. You never backed down, stayed in prayer, interceding for our family, and you never fell from grace. I know that this assignment will touch many, as it has done for me. I love you, mighty man of God. Keep doing what you do; I'm so very proud of you, and I am blessed to have witnessed the completion of this God-assigned assignment and grateful that your diligence inspired my testimonial journey along the way. #You've finished the Work!

Yours truly,
The Mrs.

CONTENTS

INTRODUCTION to "The Tree"

In this world we live in, there are so many things that hinder us from reaching the potential or fulfilling the purpose in which God has planned for us. Our natural senses are sometimes our greatest enemy; and the society we live in can make perception a reality and guide us right down the pathway to destruction. There will come a time when we'll be called to make a choice. A choice of whether we will serve God or the ways of the world. It's not easy because of the possible rejection you'll receive from family and friends, attacks on your character, or simply because you have chosen the way of Christ. I encourage you to stay the course; stay on the straight and narrow; have faith when all around you seems impossible; and trust in He that is the same yesterday, today, and forever more. Ladies and gentlemen, we present to you "The Tree"!

Supporting Scriptures

1 Corinthians 15:58 — Therefore, my beloved brothers, be steadfast, immovable, always abounding in the work of the Lord, knowing that in the Lord your labor is not in vain.

Joshua 24:14–15 — 14 "Now therefore fear the Lord and serve him in sincerity and in faithfulness. Put away the gods that your fathers served beyond the River and in Egypt, and serve the Lord. 15 And if it is evil in your eyes to serve the Lord, choose this day whom you will serve, whether the gods your fathers served in the region beyond the River, or the gods of the Amorites in whose land you dwell. But as for me and my house, we will serve the Lord."

Matthew 5:10 — Blessed are they which are persecuted for righteousness' sake: for theirs is the kingdom of heaven.

Matthew 7:13–14 — 13 "Enter by the narrow gate. For the gate is wide and the way is easy[a] that leads to destruction, and those who enter by it are many. 14 For the gate is narrow and the way is hard that leads to life, and those who find it are few.

THE TREE

I am a single tree alone in the desert.
Daily I watch a billion grains of sand
as they move about, shifting from place to place
based on the wind as it blows.

So beautiful they are to the naked eye;
but naked means uncovered or totally exposed.
Wonder if they hold that same beauty
when behind closed doors.

Ah man, should I warn all the cats
that curiosity is trying to come back,
Or should I simply close my eyes
whenever it knocks or stops by?

Dilemma:
If I close my eyes, I can't see;
forcing me to trust something greater than me.
"You know who!"
Yet if I open my eyes, it's clear to me
that even in the desert,
simple grains of sand are not what they appear to be.

There are times I feel them trying to push up against me.
Trying to force me to the left or right
as if they were in charge and telling me
"You follow, we guide."
My reply: "Whatever, bro, your voice I don't recognize."

Pay attention—
I'm the only tree in this desert amongst these grains of sand.
It hasn't always been this way,
but all the other trees were unable to stand.
For every time the strong winds would blow,
one by one, I watched them disappear into the dust.
How? When we were created and cared for the same;
wonderfully made and carefully maintained.

Check it:
My bark is healthy, and my leaves are of many colors,
My appearance does not reflect this environment
but that of my creator.
The origin of my roots, you cannot find,
no matter how deep you dig.
For it's not in the ground, but in the Word
of the one who giveth life and calls me "His."
The desert provides nothing that I need,
On the contrary, it should be the death of me.
But the water—correction—oh that living water that feeds me
comes from the river that will never run dry;
overflowing with the essentials needed for long life;
pure and holy, everlasting and ever flowing;
with a guarantee that I will thirst no more;
I will want no more, or need no more.
Wow, the revelation has been revealed to me;
Though they are many and I am but one,
I will stand amongst them all with my branches spread wide
and my posture upright.
For I'm not the only tree in this desert,
I'm just the only one that chose to stand for Christ.

INTRODUCTION to "My God"

God created man in his image and provided everything he would need to enjoy life on earth, which He also created. However, man lost his way which led to his true identity being flawed. He has struggled to uphold and fulfill the purpose for which God created him, and therefore, the world partnered with man's flesh and created a crooked and wide road that leads to the pit of hell. But thanks to God's grace and mercy that follows us even when we travel down crooked roads and dark valleys where there are shadows of death, and still be protected, and redeemed by the blood of Christ. And because of the perfection of his plan for us, we have an assurance of victory, as long as we hold on and have faith. Not only does He provide what is needed for the spirit of man, but He also provides a woman for the man, and they shall become husband and wife. He has created all things, and there is none like Him. His creation may not be what it was originally designed to be, but because of His love, faithfulness, and blood His son shed on the cross, who now sits at the right hand of the Father, gives us a hope that His children will turn from their evil ways and call on His name to be healed, saved, and become worthy of the Kingdom of Heaven. He is sovereign and just in all His ways, and even though many don't understand his thoughts or ways, or don't agree with how he moves and responds, it doesn't even matter because He will always be "My God."

Supporting Scriptures

Solomon 2:6–7 — 6 His left hand is under my head, and his right hand embraces me! 7 I adjure you, O daughters of Jerusalem by the gazelles or the does of the field, that you not stir up or awaken love until it pleases.

Jeremiah 29:11–12 — 11 For I know the plans I have for you, declares the Lord, plans for welfare and not for evil, to give you a future and a hope. 12 Then you will call upon me and come and pray to me, and I will hear you.

2 Corinthians 5:16–17 — 16 From now on, therefore, we regard no one according to the flesh. Even though we once regarded Christ according to the flesh, we regard him thus no longer. 17 Therefore, if anyone is in Christ, he is a new creation. The old has passed away; behold, the new has come.

Hebrews 11:1–3 — 1 Now faith is the assurance of things hoped for, the conviction of things not seen. 2 For by it the people of old received their commendation. 3 By faith we understand that the universe was created by the word of God, so that what is seen was not made out of things that are visible.

MY GOD

My shadow is fading, pieces scattered throughout my life.
And though the mirror reveals I'm whole,
There are parts of me that seem to be barely attached.

Like wild weeds peeking out of cracks in concrete.
Symbolic to the realization
that maybe there are certain parts of my life
I'm a little skeptical or cautious to see.
Or in some cases, want to believe.

Can a man run from himself?
All exhausted and breathing hard,
only to find that "self" is after "him."

Oh, I was created with purpose; predestined for great things;
and given authority to rule.
Do you think Adam forgot that part of the plan
after God blessed him with Eve?

The seed of Proverbs 31 planted in my life;
watered by the rains of heaven and
shined on by the true Son above;
Has now brought forth a fruit that is sweet to my lips
and a warm and gentle place to exercise my hips.

She is the definition of complete and pure;
molded and designed by the potter's hands.
His love is within her and consumes her very soul;
given to share in marriage with only this man.

While in awe, quietness overcomes—okay!
Without flaw, Almighty God comes to mind!
Without God, I find the door to my soul is wide open
and here comes that old, raggedy, no-good friend of mine.
However, old keys don't fit new locks,
and the presence of God can repel one's urgency to knock.

Check it
What is unseen is clear
and that which is seen, well, it may not be as it appears.
For the eye can only see, but the heart and mind determine what is.
For what the eyes cannot see, faith awaits its opportunity
to manifest the impossible, and reveal the evidence that
the God I serve is able, alive and well!

INTRODUCTION to "Eternal"

Some say nothing in life is forever. There's a good chance the majority would say love is a temporary thing. It's hard to imagine something being eternal, in other words, meaning without an end. When I think of eternal, the first thing comes to mind is God. We can sometimes find ourselves living in a state of sorrow, and the pain seems to never go away. This results in our actions being repeated, and the same mistakes are made over and over again, to the point we say, "It is what it is." The word of God says everything is meaningless; in other words, unless it is of God and pertains to His way, will, and word, then its value is truly nothing in the grand scheme of things. Eternal speaks to those who have found it difficult to understand the struggles and pains of life; the pains of life; addictions and neglect are only temporary if they turn it over to Christ. However, that is with the assumption one is aware of God and understands that He is the Alpha and Omega, the Beginning and the End. It is then, and only then, they can pursue those things that are eternal. Ladies and gentleman, we present to you "Eternal."

Supporting Scriptures

Psalms 136:1–3 — Give thanks to the Lord, for he is good, for his steadfast love endures forever. 2 Give thanks to the God of gods, for his steadfast love endures forever. 3 Give thanks to the Lord of lords, for his steadfast love endures forever;

Isaiah 50:10 — 10 Who among you fears the Lord and obeys the voice of his servant? Let him who walks in darkness and has no light trust in the name of the Lord and rely on his God.

Matthew 19:4–6 — "Haven't you read," he replied, "that at the beginning the Creator 'made them male and female,' and said, 'For this reason a man will leave his father and mother and be united to his wife, and the two will become one flesh'? So, they are no longer two, but one flesh. Therefore, what God has joined together, let no one separate.

John 3:16 — For God so loved the world, that he gave his only begotten Son, that whoever believes in him should not perish but have eternal life.

James 1:12 — Blessed is the man who remains steadfast under trial, for when he has stood the test he will receive the crown of life, which God has promised to those who love him.

ETERNAL

This place is dark, cold, and unfamiliar,
yet it seems very comfortable and safe.
But there's a calm voice that says to me,
"Please leave, you shouldn't be in this place."
See fear brings about caution, but caution is only temporary;
especially when curiosity knocks on the door of desire, and you answer.
Wait, wait! Didn't curiosity kill the cat? and if so,
why was the dog allowed to live?
Could it be one was looking for better while the other understood
that I'll make for the better of what I have and where I's is.

Understand—new dollar, worn dollar; still a dollar—I can spend it.
New jeans, old jeans; still a pair of jeans—I can wear them.
Okay you missed it:
New clothes become old; old clothes become worn material.
Worn material, worn material. Okay, think; sew them together.
Worn material, worn material. Okay, look; now a beautiful new quilt.
So symbolic to new love that has grown old;
carefully take the pieces that are good,
be patient in sewing them all together,
and the true beauty and power of love will be revealed
instead of what your flesh desires you to see or feel.

Please listen: Time can depreciate the value of some objects
but fortifies the foundation of love.
For love can never be measured by stuff,
but by every trial and tribulation it endures.

Okay, speak:

The level of your love will always be equal to the level of your sacrifice.
You know; For God so loved the world that He sent His only begotten son.
You know; To sacrifice His all; He was nailed to a tree,
He died for you and me and rose on day three.
What more do you need?
 "We free, we free, we free!"

Okay, I need you to get this:
A house built on the word of God does not fall
as long as the foundation of the people within are rooted in His word.
Because if you can't love through the bad,
you can't truly appreciate or understand
a love that can be defined as "Good."

Really:
No man or woman is perfect; sorry, no disrespect.
For to seek something with perfect qualities means
you can only be seeking God.
In finding God, they will understand that perfection
has been seen in one, the One, and his name is Jesus.
So, if they want or need perfection, or insecure without perfection;
they will forever be disappointed.
But if they believe God is able and faithful;
understand their desires must align with His;
have hope and trust, and remember the mustard seed;
then just as God's word is forever more, so shall be their love,
and it will be called "Eternal."

INTRODUCTION to "Who Is This God?"

Many times, we struggle with those who say they are Christians or children of God. This is solely because what we know or don't know of God, and in other cases, what is seen or reflected in their behavior or actions. They strongly display being better than or above; wiser and greater; or the only ones God can love, show compassion, have a relationship with, or welcome into His presence. It is a tragedy when this behavior is practiced, for it portrays our God in a way that doesn't honor who He truly is. "Who Is This God" will speak of such a people. Those that have created their own image or definition of the only True and Living God, and act and speak in a way that contradicts our Lord and Savior. He has not changed from the beginning of time and will not when this world comes to pass. He is "everything holy and righteous" and should never be portrayed as anything less. So now you tell me, "Who Is This God?"

Supporting Scriptures

Isaiah 29:13 — And the Lord said: "Because this people draw near with their mouth and honor me with their lips, while their hearts are far from me, and their fear of me is a commandment taught by men,

Ezekiel 33:31 — And they come to you as people come, and they sit before you as my people, and they hear what you say but they will not do it; for with lustful talk in their mouths they act; their heart is set on their gain.

Matthew 15:7–9 — 7 You hypocrites! Well did Isaiah prophesy of you, when he said: 8 "'This people honor me with their lips, but their heart is far from me; 9 in vain do they worship me teaching as doctrines the commandments of men.'"

1 Corinthians 4:4–7 — 4 For I am not aware of anything against myself, but I am not thereby acquitted. It is the Lord who judges me. 5 Therefore do not pronounce judgment before the time, before the Lord comes, who will bring to light the things now hidden in darkness and will disclose the purposes of the heart. Then each one will receive his commendation from God. 6 I have applied all these things to myself and Apollos for your benefit, brothers, that you may learn by us not to go beyond what is written, that none of you may be puffed up in favor of one against another. 7 For who sees anything different in you? What do you have that you did not receive? If then you received it, why do you boast as if you did not receive it?

WHO IS THIS GOD

Question—Who is this God you represent?
And instantly you look at me as if I'm the devil himself.
Interesting! What if I had insight into your past?
Would I find that you've asked this question as well!

Calm down, Lone Ranger, as you climb down from your high horse.
For the mask you wear, suggests in your past somewhere,
Umm, that maybe you're not telling it all.
Okay, let's not get off track;
for though I've come to you, I'm not seeking you,
nor you I desire to know.
But because I've come to you, I hope you can lead me to,
He who is the same yesterday, today, and forever more.

My apology! You seem perplexed and somewhat confused.
Are you upset because of the question I've asked you?
Never mind, lost opportunity.
Oh, and by the way, your true color is showing.
But don't worry, your secret is safe with me,
However, what is hidden in the dark is revealed by the Light.
And the Light might reveal that "You sho is ugly!"

Okay, let's try this again. Who is this God you represent?
Oh, and why I'm asking? FLASHBACK.
"Oh, I'm blessed and highly favored"; "I'm too blessed to be stressed";
"I serve a mighty God"; "He is my everything, I need for nothing";
and so on, and so on, and so on—sound familiar?

WHO IS THIS GOD YOU REPRESENT?

I'm sorry, I'm sorry, so sorry; just got a little emotional.
I apologize, for there's no need for me to yell.
But your words don't mirror your actions, and your actions, well…
they reflect and remind me of who I am now

See, I'm lost in this world without any direction,
and those who know Him treat me less than.
They quarrel about who is greater in His kingdom
based on their longevity in serving Him.
One says the glass is half empty; the other half full;
Tell me: What does that matter to the one
who has been wandering in the desert for forty years!
I'll tell you: Nothing, not a single thing.
So, while you two stand there in a negative posture towards me;
Never mind, you've lost another opportunity
To introduce one who thirsts to the Living Water.
So, I ask you again: Who is this God you represent?

INTRODUCTION to "Me"

Do I truly know who I am? One would argue we never find nor discover our true selves, because, to do that, we would have to know why we were created. We search for answers in our family history; the things in which we like and dislike; our upbringing and environment; and choices, past and present. Still, at the end of the day, we may find ourselves looking in the mirror trying to evaluate and determine who we truly are. Some say the soul is the embodiment of our whole being. But what if I don't know what's in my soul, or better yet, to whom I've given authority to rule over my soul. No palm reader or psychic can truly determine who you are because of the lines in your hands, or cards that are placed on a table. Trust me, God's creation is a little more complex than that. The one thing I've come to know is that God knew me before the foundations of the world, and formed in my mother's womb. In order for me to know who I truly am, I must consult the One who created me. I must allow Him to guide me in all things; prune me when parts of me are no longer good or needed; and constantly mold me as the potter molds the clay. This is the one and only way that I can become "Me." Ladies and gentleman, we present "Me"!

Supporting Scriptures

Jeremiah 1:4–5 — 4 Now the word of the Lord came to me, saying, 5 "Before I formed you in the womb I knew you, and before you were born I consecrated you; I appointed you a prophet to the nations."

Mark 12:41–43 — 41 And he sat down opposite the treasury and watched the people putting money into the offering box. Many rich people put in large sums. 42 And a poor widow came and put in two small copper coins, which make a penny. 43 And he called his disciples to him and said to them, "Truly, I say to you, this poor widow has put in more than all those who are contributing to the offering box.

Romans 7:19–25 — 19 For I do not do the good I want, but the evil I do not want is what I keep on doing. 20 Now if I do what I do not want, it is no longer I who do it, but sin that dwells within me. 21 So I find it to be a law that when I want to do right, evil lies close at hand. 22 For I delight in the law of God, in my inner being, 23 but I see in my members another law waging war against the law of my mind and making me captive to the law of sin that dwells in my members. 24 Wretched man that I am! Who will deliver me from this body of death? 25 Thanks be to God through Jesus Christ our Lord! So then, I myself serve the law of God with my mind, but with my flesh I serve the law of sin.

Romans 8:28 —And we know that for those who love God all things work together for good, for those who are called according to his purpose.

Galatians 5:1 — For freedom Christ has set us free; stand firm therefore, and do not submit again to a yoke of slavery.

ME

It reluctantly waits, pondering while looking over the horizon.
Wondering if it should introduce itself to the world.
The journey hasn't been easy, for many times it tried to escape,
but low self-esteem and fear always seem to block its pathway.
Have you ever felt paralyzed while having full use of your body parts?
Have you ever felt victimized because you're not allowed to express your thoughts?

CHECK THIS:
Feelings without expression are as useless as the world without Christ.
Christ without the cross—well, strike three.
Game over—we've all lost.

NOW UNDERSTAND THIS:
Joy and happiness have always been allowed to do whatever they want.
Like a rich man who oppresses and mistreats the less fortunate;
yet is still highly esteemed simply because of his net worth.
"The dollar, dollar bill, y'all."

Isn't it amazing how the value of something works.
The penny is larger than the dime, but its value is less.
Try telling that to the man who doesn't have a penny to his name.
Now the nickel is larger than the penny and is shining like new money,
but it will tuck its tail and run at the drop of a dime.
Man, you ain't worth a quarter!

Something has to give or the bow will surely break.
For things naturally released shouldn't have to try and escape.
You do remember the children of Egypt—God's Chosen!
You do remember who God sent to free them—Brother Moses!

You do remember that they were released with treasures—Loaded!
You know He can do the same for you if you let Him—The Inheritance!
Still afraid to get out of the boat,
even though you're sitting on dry land.
A captive to your own insecurities that have somehow
become your security.
Better check the locks on your doors;
make sure the keys you have are yours;
make sure a set has been given to the One above;
so that He can come and go as He pleases;
so He can lock out the things that do not please Him.

Selah—
If I hide something, does it become the hidden?
Or if I forgive someone, do they become the forgiven?
What if I die to something, does that mean I'm no longer living?
Umm, the way I see it is:
What is hidden must come in from hiding so that it may be seen.
And the forgiven must learn how to forgive, otherwise by God they won't be
cleaned.
Oh, and the living must die to some things in order to live a life for the King.

What are you trying to say?
There's someone that wants to live,
yet restrained because they don't trust the power inside of them.
That power which has authority to release;
open and close doors, remove shackles and set free.

Have you ever wondered why the caged bird sings?
Could it be because its freedom is from within?
Or, maybe that it has accepted that "it is what it is?"
Either way, it keeps on singing that "Same Ole Song!"

Know this:

Open a freezer in the desert; the ice will be set free.

Open a freezer in the Antarctic and without choice, the ice cannot leave.

Understand that freedom will always come with a price.

God proved that when he sent his Only Begotten as a sacrifice.

and the Only Begotten understood and willingly gave up His life.

I can hear the caged bird singing,

And this time I refuse to ignore its song.

For its melody, though it sounds sweet, masks the lyrics that say

"This cage is not my home."

This is your lucky day, caged bird, I'm setting you free

Which means that I'm also setting someone else free—ME!

INTRODUCTION to "Church Folks"

Quick to judge and condemn, and turn their noses up at those who don't look or speak like them. They praise and worship in the house of God and have come to believe they set the rules and standards, forgetting that before God found them, they were just as filthy as those they now despise. It has become a club only the so-called "holy" can be privy to, and they treat those they feel are not up to their standards with such ungodliness, that "holy" has a whole new definition. They are supposed to be the ones that are not judgmental; that forgive and show compassion; willing to lend a helping hand and not bias but impartial; and ambassadors and representatives of the Most-High God. It is no longer a mystery to me why the world feels the way they do toward the church, and it is very saddening that the church as a whole is being blamed. So, let me be clear! It's not the church, but instead, it's the "Church Folks." Ladies and gentlemen, we present to you, "Church Folks."

Supporting Scriptures

Isaiah 53:3 — He was despised and rejected by men, a man of sorrows and acquainted with grief; and as one from whom men hide their faces he was despised, and we esteemed him not.

Matthew 25:40–45 — 40 And the King will answer them, 'Truly, I say to you, as you did it to one of the least of these my brothers, you did it to me.' 41 "Then he will say to those on his left, 'Depart from me, you cursed, into the eternal fire prepared for the devil and his angels. 42 For I was hungry and you gave me no food, I was thirsty and you gave me no drink, 43 I was a stranger and you did not welcome me, naked and you did not clothe me, sick and in prison and you did not visit me.' 44 Then they also will answer, saying, 'Lord, when did we see you hungry or thirsty or a stranger or naked or sick or in prison, and did not minister to you?' 45 Then he will answer them, saying,

'Truly, I say to you, as you did not do it to one of the least of these, you did not do it to me.'

Luke 18:11–14 — 11 The Pharisee, standing by himself, prayed thus: 'God, I thank you that I am not like other men, extortioners, unjust, adulterers, or even like this tax collector. 12 I fast twice a week; I give tithes of all that I get.' 13 But the tax collector, standing far off, would not even lift up his eyes to heaven, but beat his breast, saying, 'God, be merciful to me, a sinner!' 14 I tell you, this man went down to his house justified, rather than the other. For everyone who exalts himself will be humbled, but the one who humbles himself will be exalted."

1 Peter 2:4–5 — 4 As you come to him, a living stone rejected by men but in the sight of God chosen and precious, 5 you yourselves like living stones are being built up as a spiritual house, to be a holy priesthood, to offer spiritual sacrifices acceptable to God through Jesus Christ.

CHURCH FOLKS

The soles of my shoes are worn down
and my lips resemble a dirt road dried by the scorching sun.
My eyes no longer guide me, for the decisions they've led me to make, well,
let's just say, I'm better off blind.

My appearance causes one to pause, unsure of what they see,
or what they think they see, or maybe,
that which resides inside of them has labeled me to be.
Yet I stand in the presence of them, and my flesh says to me, "Run."
Yet something greater tells me, "This is where you belong."

There's a stench that causes their breathing to stumble.
It aggressively approaches them from my direction;
Eyes looking me up and down—big eyes, little eyes, bubble eyes,
but none worse than condemning eyes.
Total disgust portrayed in their frowns as if I'm nothing more than a filthy
old rag.
I can hear every word they say even though their lips are lifeless.
Lifeless not because they are not speaking,
but because of what it is they are speaking.
Again, I turn to run—
Again, something greater tells me, "This is where you belong."

Quietly I take a step and my movement puts them at unease.
Now the look of fear and uncertainty has appeared.
And for every action there is a reaction;
and their reaction has confused and overwhelmed me.
'Cause what I thought was, is not what it seems to be;
Where I thought I was, didn't feel like shelter to me;

And who I thought they were, didn't reflect him that I seek.
Here I go again, prepared to turn and run,
But this time, something grabs me and says:

"This is the place where you belong and those which you've encountered
will be no more; simply put—gone.
For weeds shall be pulled and only my flowers remain;
and my temple will be cleansed and occupied by those once stained.
For this is the shelter for the many lost sheep.
Those who have wandered in the wilderness, rejected by those claiming to
be of me.
So, stand still, for I have called you into my house.
A place where one finds refuge from the hatred and judgment of the world;
from the shame and guilt of who you once were; for the gift of love that is
perfect and true;
and the power of the blood that can save you.
So, let not man hinder your steps or validate your heavenly worth.
For I have called you to come to me, because what you seek,
only I and I alone, have the power to give unto thee."

INTRODUCTION to "Why Me"

I truly believe with all my heart that you find true love only once in your lifetime. This love will endure all things and meet all your needs. Throughout your life, you will experience different levels of love. Love of your first girlfriend; love of your best friend; love of your family; and love of your enemies. However, when this love shows its face, it will take you to a place you've never been before. It will arrest your heart and cause you to throw up your hands and surrender. It will reveal your weaknesses and at the same time, give you strength. It will also provide insight to someone other than yourself and reveal that love is to be shared between two under the watchful eye of God. However, it is not without struggles or adversity; tears and nights of pain; and self-sacrifice and compromise. But when it's over, it will rise like the morning sun and shine brightly upon you. No one is deserving of this love, and no one can claim they have earned it by their own works or it's owed to them. It is by God's grace and love which he plants within our hearts to share with that special someone. I have been blessed with that special someone who I truly believe was created especially for me to share love and cherish for a lifetime. As each day passes, I find myself asking God, "Why me?" Ladies and gentlemen, we present to you "Why Me."

Supporting Scriptures

Solomon 4:9 — You have captivated my heart, my sister, my bride; you have captivated my heart with one glance of your eyes, with one jewel of your necklace.

Solomon 8:6–7 — 6 Set me as a seal upon your heart, as a seal upon your arm, for love is strong as death, jealousy is fierce as the grave. Its flashes are flashes of fire, the very flame of the Lord. 7 Many waters cannot quench love, neither can floods drown it. If a man offered for love all the wealth of his house, he would be utterly despised.

Ecclesiastes 4:9 — Two are better than one, because they have a good reward for their toil.

Ecclesiastes 4:12 — And though a man might prevail against one who is alone, two will withstand him — a threefold cord is not quickly broken.

1 Corinthians 13:4–13 — 4 Love is patient and kind; love does not envy or boast; it is not arrogant 5 or rude. It does not insist on its own way; it is not irritable or resentful; 6 it does not rejoice at wrongdoing, but rejoices with the truth. 7 Love bears all things, believes all things, hopes all things, endures all things. 8 Love never ends. As for prophecies, they will pass away; as for tongues, they will cease; as for knowledge, it will pass away. 9 For we know in part and we prophesy in part, 10 but when the perfect comes, the partial will pass away. 11 When I was a child, I spoke like a child, I thought like a child, I reasoned like a child. When I became a man, I gave up childish ways. 12 For now we see in a mirror dimly, but then face to face. Now I know in part; then I shall know fully, even as I have been fully known. 13 So now faith, hope, and love abide, these three; but the greatest of these is love.

1 John 4:16 — So we have come to know and to believe the love that God has for us. God is love, and whoever abides in love abides in God, and God abides in him.

WHY ME

A glimmer of hope shows its face
while trust waits to see if it is embraced.
Is it caution that she is putting on display?
Or is it fear of what can possibly be taken away.
So timidly she plays the "soul mate" card again,
but she will not be denied.
For little joker, big joker, I have them both in my hand.

See, precious diamonds are not as rare as they seem;
but a union built on God's love, tell me, how often is that seen?

My life unfinished, and yet complete.
Speaking of what is yet to come, based on what God has already called
to be.

So, I find my mind trying to swim upstream
while the currents of doubt try to push me away from my destiny.
My destiny, my destiny—no, disregard.
His destiny, because it is perfect, not flawed.
For overzealous actions are birthed by one's emotions,
whereas acts of wisdom are birthed from God's kingdom.

Case and point:
To her, I still share and display love in the midst of my anger,
but to show her love is predicated on what controls my anger.

Think about it:
If anger is consumed by love, there my Father abides;
but if anger is consumed by hatred, there my Father can't reside.

For what is of God can't be of anything else;
you know, pure joy, peace, and eternal happiness.
Just as the gift He created to share love with me,
and who she truly is, I've been given eyes to see.

Her pain when it's unspoken, strength when she seems broken.
Her joy when tears are falling; her spiritual gifts and her calling.
Her hand that is designed to fit mine, and her beauty at mornings first light.
So as the sun turns its back and walks away from the day;
the moon lights its candle and takes its place.

I find myself in awe and grateful of my gift from above,
and I humbly look to the heavens and say to my Father,
"What an amazing love to share—*Why me?*"

INTRODUCTION to "Truly"

It is not hard to lose yourself when everything and everyone around desires you to be this or that. Daily we find ourselves portraying something we once despised, but because of society, and our desire to fit in, we dress and act the part. There is an old saying that you are the company you keep, but what I've come to learn is that I become the company I keep, simply because the flesh is weak and my strong desire for others to accept me. Strength is found in the one who understands who and what they are according to God and live within the commands and statutes of His holy word. The world provides us with the opportunity to have no responsibility unto ourselves, but mostly, unto God. It's a playground without rules and limitations, and if you aren't careful, you will completely lose sight of who you are; I mean, who you *truly* are! Ladies and gentlemen, we present to you, "Truly."

Supporting Scriptures

Psalms 51:10–12 — 10 Create in me a clean heart, O God, and renew a right spirit within me. 11 Cast me not away from your presence, and take not your Holy Spirit from me. 12 Restore to me the joy of your salvation, and uphold me with a willing spirit.

Matthew 23:28 — So you also outwardly appear righteous to others, but within you are full of hypocrisy and lawlessness.

2 Corinthians 4:16–18 — 16 So we do not lose heart. Though our outer self is wasting away, our inner self is being renewed day by day. 17 For this light momentary affliction is preparing for us an eternal weight of glory beyond all comparison, 18 as we look not to the things that are seen but to the things that are unseen. For the things that are seen are transient, but the things that are unseen are eternal.

2 Corinthians 5:17 — Therefore, if anyone is in Christ, he is a new creation. The old has passed away; behold, the new has come.

Ephesians 4:20–24 — 20 But that is not the way you learned Christ! 21 assuming that you have heard about him and were taught in him, as the truth is in Jesus, 22 to put off your old self, which belongs to your former manner of life and is corrupt through deceitful desires, 23 and to be renewed in the spirit of your minds, 24 and to put on the new self, created after the likeness of God in true righteousness and holiness.

James 1:23–25 — 23 For if anyone is a hearer of the word and not a doer, he is like a man who looks intently at his natural face in a mirror. 24 For he looks at himself and goes away and at once forgets what he was like. 25 But the one who looks into the perfect law, the law of liberty, and perseveres, being no hearer who forgets but a doer who acts, he will be blessed in his doing.

James 4:4 — You adulterous people! Do you not know that friendship with the world is enmity with God? Therefore whoever wishes to be a friend of the world makes himself an enemy of God.

TRULY

My thoughts are lifeless like the rose that could no longer breathe in the snow.

And because its color has not faded, it gives false hope to those who don't know.

That life doesn't always reflect one's appearance,

and one's appearance doesn't always reflect one's condition.

Yeah, I've perfected my smile;

and the clothes I wear say, "I must be a man of importance."

Now include my portrayal of supreme confidence; and the people say,

"That brother wants for nothing."

WRONG!

Because a mask is very cheap, and on a good day,

you can buy one and get one free—BOGO!

Problem is this:

If you wear a mask long enough, you forget it's on.

If you wear a mask long enough, your own face becomes unknown.

See, to your human eye my portrait is authentic,

but to the One who can see beyond the canvas

knows that what I want you to see and believe,

well, simply put, it's counterfeit.

False, misleading, just simply an act;

rehearsed so much, that to me it's become a fact.

Remove me from the stage, observe me from afar;

as the make-up is removed, you'll see the many scars.

Yet my pain can't be reflected in a mirror;

but somehow Joy saw it, packed up and left; go figure.

Enough about me, back to the rose.

Why was the rose found lifeless in the snow?

Was it running from something; trying to find something;

trying to be something; or was it up to something "no good"?

Nevertheless, choices have consequences,

but based on what one is in need of,
consequences can become the least of.
And by that we justify; become like clay, molded to look like;
bury memories of past generations' sacrifices;
and learn to act and talk according to what the world likes.

My decisions proven to be reckless with my behavior, screaming, "Please help me!"
For who I truly am can't be what I think I am;
for who I truly am is determined by "I Am that I Am";
which is greater than the man the world says I am.

Pause.... quietly speak:
If I allow the world to define me, I am according to many.
Yet if I'm defined by He that created all things,
then and only then, can I be called "Authentic."

Okay…
I've thrown my masks away, didn't sell them on eBay.
For I would never support or encourage another
to hide behind the truth of one's self;
just to be accepted and please everyone else.
I retraced the steps of the rose;
eyes full of tears because the steps led to my door.
And inside, by the vase a letter was placed
that spoke of a man that wore a mask over his face.

It read:
I pray you hear the voice of God
and remember you are fearfully and wonderfully made.
That who you are and everything you do should be pleasing unto God,
and to the world, gladly portrayed.
I'll always love you for the home you provided;

the home in which the Holy Spirit once resided.
But as it departed, so did I;
and I've been searching for it every day and night.
So, if you ever find me, trust that God's spirit is there as well.
And I will find rest, oh that wonderful rest;
for in the presence of my Father, again I will rejoice and dwell—Truly.

INTRODUCTION to "Faded Jeans"

Normally when you think of something that is faded, immediately you believe it has been extensively worn or used over a period of time. This goes to speak to one's life and journey. There is nothing wrong with being a little worn out from the trials and tribulations of life. In many cases, things that are worn or have been used hold more value than things that are new. This speaks to past traditions and family values. This also speaks to the roles and responsibilities of those who are God's children. Normally, when something fades away it doesn't immediately disappear. However, what remains as one begins to fade doesn't seem to hold the same value as it once did. "Faded Jeans" speaks to those who believe that their value is based on what is now and current, and not that which has brought them through the stormy rains and valley lows. Our prayer is, as you read this, you will know God can use anything for His purpose. Also, your value and worth can never be measured by what is, but mostly by what you've become because of what was. So, if you've looked into your closet and feel you need a new pair of jeans, I urge you to reconsider, because who and what you are, and your worth will still be the same, even if you put on them "Faded Jeans."

Supporting Scriptures

Psalms 23:1–6 — 1 The Lord is my shepherd; I shall not want. 2 He makes me lie down in green pastures. He leads me beside still waters. 3 He restores my soul. He leads me in paths of righteousness for his name's sake. 4 Even though I walk through the valley of the shadow of death, I will fear no evil, for you are with me; your rod and your staff, they comfort me. 5 You prepare a table before me in the presence of my enemies; you anoint my head with oil; my cup overflows. 6 Surely goodness and mercy shall follow me all the days of my life, and I shall dwell in the house of the Lord forever.

John 14:12–13 — 12 "Truly, truly, I say to you, whoever believes in me will also do the works that I do; and greater works than these will he do, because I am going to the Father. 13 Whatever you ask in my name, this I will do, that the Father may be glorified in the Son.

Luke 5:36–39 — 36 He also told them a parable: "No one tears a piece from a new garment and puts it on an old garment. If he does, he will tear the new, and the piece from the new will not match the old. 37 And no one puts new wine into old wineskins. If he does, the new wine will burst the skins and it will be spilled, and the skins will be destroyed. 38 But new wine must be put into fresh wineskins. 39 And no one after drinking old wine desires new, for he says, 'The old is good.'"

2 Corinthians 5:7 — for we walk by faith, not by sight.

1 Timothy 4:4–5 — 4 For everything created by God is good, and nothing is to be rejected if it is received with thanksgiving, 5 for it is made holy by the word of God and prayer.

Hebrews 4:12–13 — 12 For the word of God is living and active, sharper than any two-edged sword, piercing to the division of soul and of spirit, of joints and of marrow, and discerning the thoughts and intentions of the heart. 13 And no creature is hidden from his sight, but all are naked and exposed to the eyes of him to whom we must give account.

FADED JEANS

I've watched her color fade like jeans that have been washed too many times,
yet the fabric of her being remains.
Still, I question whether the threads have the integrity to hold everything
together,
or better yet, the strength to bind.

For her secret is out, true identity now revealed,
Which has drawn out another whose identity, though well known,
has somehow been concealed.
Hidden in plain sight, but only to the spiritually blind.
I apologize! Let me correct myself, also those with worldly minds.

Okay, spiritually speaking:
One's purpose is found in God's calling,
and one's gifts are perfected through God's Spirit.
This is the guarantee that you were created with purpose,
and spiritual gifts to do mighty and wonderful things.

Tell me, then, why aren't you confident enough to wear those faded jeans?

I'll tell you this:
It's a tragedy when life is taken. Even worse, to give up on life while still
breathing.
Take one breath, two breaths, three breaths—give thanks to the One who
giveth life.
Now four breaths, five breaths, six breaths—give praise to the One who
shows grace and mercy.

By now it should be easier to continue breathing. I'm sorry, living.

'Cause for every breath you breathe;
He breathes it into you so you can give Him the honor and glory.
Tell Me:
Who ran you off the road called "The Straight and Narrow"?
Who told you there was no light in the valley?
And that you can't sit at the table because your enemies are present?
Oh, and who told you that the blood He shed was not for you?
Better yet, I'm not greatly concerned about who told you,
but I'm more concerned because you believed.

See what we believe is mostly based on what we see,
and what we see governs how we process and perceive.
Make a choice: Eyesight that's 20/20;
Or be blind and led by God's Holy Spirit?

So, let me answer the Who questions:
About the straight and narrow: Well, you did!
For it was easy for you to move around on the crooked and wide.
Oh, no light in the valley: You did!
When you trusted your eyes and abandoned your faith.
Ah, can't sit at the table: You did!
When your fear became your master.
And that the blood of Christ was not for you: You did!
When you allowed sin to condemn you.
Change doesn't occur until one can acknowledge their faults.
Just like one can't be found until they acknowledge they're lost.

Now who's flying this plane? They say his name is Pride,
and his co-pilot "Flesh" is dressed to the tee and thinking he is funky fresh!
Trust me when I say, you don't wanna roll with these brothers.

Their flight plan flawed, credentials unqualified.
Might wanna check your itinerary,

'Cause the destination of this flight is the "Lake of Fire."

Now, do you smell something burning?
My apologies, didn't mean to be so brunt,
But the word is sharper than any double-edged sword.
It should pierce, cut and divide;
Peel away the flesh; reveal those things you want to hide.
"Peekaboo—I see you!"

Now you come on from behind them trees.
Why you hiding when you should be seeking?
What happened to you that stopped you from believing?

Oh! Are you mad because He didn't answer your call?

Selah
Check yourself—How you gonna expect him to answer your call
when you refused to answer His calling?
All in yourself while yourself is trying to find a way out.
It's tired of hearing only your voice, tired of being lost,
So, it's gnawing and scratching at the door; desperately seeking a way out.

The door is opened, your eyes gaze upon glory;
there Jesus is standing, with his arms extended;
time is temporarily suspended, your mind trying to comprehend it.
Is this the end? He says no, it's the beginning;
you begin confessing, He begins forgiving.
The world becomes your enemy; you lose some friends and family;
but He fulfills, and you lack nothing.
Renews your mind, gives you wisdom;
and prepares you for eternal life in the kingdom.
Transforms you into who He desires you to be;
Giving you the strength and courage to wear them faded jeans.

INTRODUCTION to "Doing It Wrong!"

"Doing It Wrong" was birthed when our youngest son went off to college. One day we woke up and our home, once filled with friendly banter and serious life conversations, had been replaced with silence. The two of us looking at one another with deer-in-the-headlight eyes while questioning, what do we do now? We'd become parents at the ripe ages of twenty and twenty-two and had grown accustomed to the hustle and bustle of being parents of active kids. Life as we'd known it had been changed. Although we had celebrated our eighteenth wedding anniversary a few months earlier, we found ourselves in the honeymoon stage of marriage all over again. Sadly coming to the realization that we had programmed ourselves to be well adept at taking care of our children and even one another; we had somehow forgotten how to take care of ourselves. If you are an empty-nester, a caregiver, caring for an aging parent, or a disabled loved one, please let "Doing It Wrong" serve as a reminder to love that which is placed in your care, and don't forget to give yourself a little tender, loving care (TLC) along the way. You can only be great for others if you are great for yourself first, physically, mentally, and spiritually.

Supporting Scripture

Romans 12:2 —Do not be conformed to this world, but be transformed by the renewal of your mind, that by testing you may discern what is the will of God, what is good and acceptable and perfect.

1 Corinthians 6:19 —Do you not know your body is a temple of the Holy Spirit, who is in you, whom you have received from God

Ladies and gentlemen, we present "Doing It Wrong."

DOING IT WRONG

Taking care of everyone else for so long;
finally realizing you've been doing it wrong
Setting aside your own aspirations
with hopes that everyone else's dreams will come to fruition.

Thoughts creeping in about your life when they're grown;
perhaps a different scenario, your life when they're gone,
realizing for sure that you've been doing it wrong!

Will that leave me alone, all alone? Maya said, "Nobody,
but nobody can make it all alone."

I put on a happy face trying to disguise my true feelings;
pain, hurt, that's what's inside me. Wondering my purpose or if I'll meet my
demise with God-given gifts that just fell by the wayside.

The good Lord knows I don't wanna be that chic, after all he made me awe-
some and topped me off with a little grit.

Two doors with different pathways. Door "A," self-destruct and waddle in
misery;
Door "B," roll away the stone and fulfill my purpose-filled destiny.

I'm screaming loudly from a mountain top, yes, I'm "DYNAMITE!" While
trying to keep it all together to prove I got my shit tight.

Pride comes before destruction, is what the good book says; sometimes it's
easier said than done when there is so much at stake. I can't wait too long to
course-correct from all of my mistakes.

My light shines brightest only when it's turned on. This equation does not include being all alone.
Guess I'd better get off the boat, dive in and hope for a jolt.

Time stands still for no one; catch up or be frozen in time. Admitting your faults and swallowing your pride, knowing it's your time to live your best life; no longer doing wrong but doing it ALL right!

INTRODUCTION to "The Man Within"

What and who defines a man? Truth is, it's impossible to conclude because of the vast number of variables in the world. However, when it comes to what a man is according to God, well, that is crystal clear, but only to those who know the Word. Find a man with a gentle heart and one would call him soft or a pushover. Find a man that speaks his mind no matter whom it hurts, then some would call him strong. It bewilders me how the world has become the validation of who we are and not the creator. The Man Within speaks to the trials and tribulations of living according to God or that of the world. It portrays one who is struggling to hold on because his flesh is fighting to be set free. There is a power that we've been blessed with that's a gift from our Father—the Holy Spirit. This is the only thing that should guide and direct us in all things. This is what will determine the man within. Ladies and gentlemen, we present to you "The Man Within"!

Supporting Scriptures

Ezekiel 36:27 — And I will put my Spirit within you, and cause you to walk in my statutes and be careful to obey my rules.

John 14:16–17 — 16 And I will ask the Father, and he will give you another Helper, to be with you forever, 17 even the Spirit of truth, whom the world cannot receive, because it neither sees him nor knows him. You know him, for he dwells with you and will be in you.

1 Corinthians 6:19–20 — 19 Or do you not know that your body is a temple of the Holy Spirit within you, whom you have from God? You are not your own, 20 for you were bought with a price. So, glorify God in your body.

2 Timothy 1:14 — By the Holy Spirit who dwells within us, guard the good deposit entrusted to you.

Titus 3:4–7 — 4 But when the goodness and loving kindness of God our Savior appeared, 5 he saved us, not because of works done by us in righteousness, but according to his own mercy, by the washing of regeneration and renewal of the Holy Spirit, 6 whom he poured out on us richly through Jesus Christ our Savior, 7 so that being justified by his grace we might become heirs according to the hope of eternal life.

THE MAN WITHIN

Wanting to scream at the top of my lungs, "To hell with it, I'm so tired!"
What was in my reserve no longer remains;
truth be told, don't know what's keeping me upright.

A product of a long line of strong men.
Not perfect in any way, but strong in the sense of
what I believe it takes to be a man.
So much weight that one must bear,
find myself wanting to just release a little here,
a little there, a little wherever,
Now I'm in that bad place; really beginning not to care.

Find a man without a purpose,
and there you'll find a man who is wandering in the wilderness.
For without purpose there is nothing to conquer.
And when there's nothing to conquer,
he'll create something to conquer, or someone.
A warrior by nature but gentle in and through the spirit.
Be careful not to force him to eat from that tree, for then he'll know he's naked.
He'll hide what must be hidden, and lie to conceal that which is forbidden.
Now we have a problem!

It's a fine line between love and hate.
It's an even finer line between honor and disrespect.
Question is: Which side of these lines are you on?
Remember no one can straddle the fence because when you do,
well, what has the strongest pull will win every time.
Lost in one's self, beginning to rest in self-preservation.
Feeling a slight touch on the shoulder and hearing someone say:

"Tell them how you really feel!"
And what's in your heart finally sees the exit,
and rushes right out of your mouth "buck naked."

Sometimes I can feel the wind pushing,
and my mind wonders if it's trying to guide me somewhere.
Reminds me of this voice I always hear
that holds me from destroying the things in which I deeply care.
Yet lately an old friend has come back to visit,
surprisingly he has brought along some of his friends.
My eyes sharply focused on them, they look a'ight,
but there's that voice again, so calm, yet powerful enough
to give one the strength to say, "Not ta-night!"

My arms are tired, feel my grip slowly fading.
My thoughts are unfriendly, low down and shady.
My strength is minimal, don't know if I can hold this weight.
And my compassion has packed it bags,
contemplating whether it will go or stay.
My will depleted, happiness in hiding,
My understanding still wants to talk,
but my anger won't let him.
Hell, who am I fooling, I'm an utter mess!

But hold on…
Whenever one is at his lowest, he has a better picture of who's on high.
It is this place I'm closest to Him; that His voice is clearer to me.
Leading me to a place where there is one on a stool;
Where the table has been set, and His hands are the tools.
It is me He's awaiting; at this moment all things start changing.
For I'm at the Potter's house and about to have Him lay his hands on me.
"You can do to me whatever you like!"

Totally transformed for this appointed time;
to only be transformed again for the final time—resurrected.
So how can I be and not be myself at the same time?
My face looks the same and my body does as well;
haven't grown an inch, that includes my hair, as far as I can tell.
A brother feeling pretty good about himself.
My arms are rested, grip stronger than ever;
thoughts filled with love and life.

My strength is no longer mine, but in and through Christ;
"I can do all things through Christ who strengthens me."
Compassion unpacked its bag, found out it has a room of its own.
My will remained depleted, no worries—no value,
'cause I chose the Master's and not my own.
Now understanding has a brand-new walk after it put anger in its place.
And me, well, that utter mess has a new housekeeper and trust me when I say:
This brother can walk on water.

So, who I was is no longer, and what was weak has become much stronger.
My past or current state only has the power I give it,
and life is about what I believe according to Him my soul I've submitted.

Check this:
Choices and decisions are such a beauty to possess;
yet they can lead to such ugly results.
Trust in that which is greater than you, He that is without sin.
He that is perfect in all His ways and was beaten for you.
He that carried His own cross, to later give up His life for you.
Let everything go!
Just let it all go and give everything to Him,
and receive only that which He has given,
Then, and only then, you'll know what it is to be free.

INTRODUCTION to "Internal Heat"

A cold heart is the resident of many ugly and ungodly things. There you will find jealousy, envy, hatred, bitterness, fornication, adultery, and love of the world. It's a condition in which God never intended for the heart, and it's a place where the joy of life is lost. The heart is at the center of all things. It's by which we are judged and where the flow of nasty and disrespectful words originates. It is the place in which temptation resides, waiting for someone to open the door and set it free. Yet in the midst of the many ugly things of a cold heart, there is someone that is able to unthaw and provide a warmth that will bring you true peace and joy. A warmth that will open your eyes to the beauty of God's grace and mercy and peace He desires for all His children. It doesn't cost you anything except that you open your heart and allow Him to enter. And once He has entered, I would suggest you give Him a key and make Him the doorkeeper. There will be no room for the cold because as long as He is there, you will receive the internal heat from His spirit. Ladies and gentlemen, we hope you enjoy "Internal Heat"!

Supporting Scriptures

Proverbs 27:19 — As in water, face reflects face, so the heart of man reflects the man.

Psalms 51:10 — Create in me a clean heart, O God, and renew a right spirit within me.

Ezekiel 36:26 — And I will give you a new heart, and a new spirit I will put within you. And I will remove the heart of stone from your flesh and give you a heart of flesh.

Mark 7:21–23 — 21 For from within, out of the heart of man, come evil thoughts, sexual immorality, theft, murder, adultery, 22 coveting, wickedness, deceit, sensuality, envy, slander, pride, foolishness. 23 All these evil things come from within, and they defile a person.

Hebrews 10:22 — let us draw near with a true heart in full assurance of faith, with our hearts sprinkled clean from an evil conscience and our bodies washed with pure water.

INTERNAL HEAT

The ice under my feet refuses to melt even though the sun is looking down on it.
Maybe a brother needs to check his own temperature.
For when cold meets cold, nothing changes.
But when cold meets the Son, things slowly begin to dissolve away.

Drip by drip, stubbornly creeping along,
not in a rush, for many years this has been its home.
So, it's constantly looking back, checking to see if I'm still chilling with the Son.
Look at him; not happy with the one who calls me friend.

We had a good relationship.
I could do whatever I wanted without restriction.
And though I was freezing to death, it convinced me that I was warm.
And though I've done many things that weren't right,
it assured me I had done nothing wrong.
"This brother ain't nothing but a snake in the grass,"
or should I say in the garden.

Freeze a body at the right temperature and some believe one can be revived later.
Yet when unthawed, if the heart is still cold,
well, no worries, there's a fire that'll still be waiting.

Back to the ice that was under my feet, chilling like it didn't have anywhere to be.
I guess I wasn't any better, for I'm the one that provided the food and shelter.

Nothing worse than housing and feeding something that wanted me dead,
or befriending an animal of the wild.

You may think it's your friend or homie, but at the appropriate time,
it will remind you of who and what it really is.

See a predator seeks out its prey while the prey runs and hide;
that's the response of the world.
That same predator can seek out its prey, but this prey stands still and pray;
now that's the response of the believer.

You do remember Daniel in the lion's den or when Saul was hunting David.
What about David and Goliath or Jesus being tempted in the wilderness,
or Jesus on the Cross: Father, please forgive them for they know not that
they do.

Okay:
How I act and live, speak and respond, love and hate,
and whom I'll serve is from within.
And how I'll be judged when it's all over,
well, that, too, is based on what's within.

Check this:
The ice is no longer relevant; no longer under my feet.
Not that I can't see it, for it's always watching me.
Problem is, there is a heat that it fears radiating from me.
So, I walk boldly with a renewed authority, but my steps can't be traced,
for they fit perfectly in the footprints of the One that goes before me.
So, what was cold no longer resides in me,
for God has filled me with His Spirit, that Internal Heat.

INTRODUCTION to "The Plan"

There is a strong desire to satisfy the flesh which causes turbulence in one's life when they decide they're going to live for Christ. We live with the flesh every day and very seldom live within the Spirit of God. Therefore, when one decides to give his life over to Christ, the war between flesh and Spirit begins. Our senses: sight, hearing, smell, taste, and touch can be a detriment to living a spiritual life, but there is another thing that is far greater—our desires, will, and way. When you relinquish your life to Christ, you are basically giving up these things for His. This is basically dying to yourself in order to live in and through Him. Giving up the things that we feel make us who we are takes a greater toll when we have riches and high-valued, material things. Also, the lack of freedom to live however we want without restrictions is hard to adjust to, or even forfeit, causing one to straddle the fence. When in this position, you are not halfway with God and the world; instead, you are of the world. In order for God to move in one's life to fulfill his purpose, that individual has to come unto him and make themselves available. Not half-committed but fully committed. There will be stumbling blocks along the way and mountains and hills to climb, but trust me—if God has called you, rest assure, you are well able and equipped to do it. He knew you before you were formed in your mother's womb, and He has "The Plan"!

Supporting Scriptures

Jeremiah 29:11 — For I know the plans I have for you, declares the Lord, plans for welfare and not for evil, to give you a future and a hope.

Proverbs 3:5–6 — 5 Trust in the Lord with all your heart, and do not lean on your own understanding. 6 In all your ways acknowledge him, and he will make straight your paths.

Proverbs 19:21 — Many are the plans in the mind of a man, but it is the purpose of the Lord that will stand.

Isaiah 58:11 — And the Lord will guide you continually and satisfy your desire in scorched places and make your bones strong; and you shall be like a watered garden, like a spring of water, whose waters do not fail.

Romans 7:14–24 — 14 For we know that the law is spiritual, but I am of the flesh, sold under sin. 15 For I do not understand my own actions. For I do not do what I want, but I do the very thing I hate. 16 Now if I do what I do not want, I agree with the law, that it is good. 17 So now it is no longer I who do it, but sin that dwells within me. 18 For I know that nothing good dwells in me, that is, in my flesh. For I have the desire to do what is right, but not the ability to carry it out. 19 For I do not do the good I want, but the evil I do not want is what I keep on doing. 20 Now if I do what I do not want, it is no longer I who do it, but sin that dwells within me. 21 So I find it to be a law that when I want to do right, evil lies close at hand. 22 For I delight in the law of God, in my inner being, 23 but I see in my members another law waging war against the law of my mind and making me captive to the law of sin that dwells in my members. 24 Wretched man that I am! Who will deliver me from this body of death?

THE PLAN

My hands are shaking so badly that the ground under my feet tremors.
Sadly, I've come to realize what I've long denied,
that maybe I'm no better than those who crucified Him.
I may not have been there or said the words, or the one with the hammer in his hand.
Yet my actions are like those in whom He chose
to ask God to forgive before fulfilling the perfect plan.

Never been blinded while traveling down a road, though I traveled many with ill intentions.
Never spent time inside of a fish; ate a few for being disobedient to God's instructions.
Spent some time with friends in my den, only later to find out they were lions.
Won't bad mouth Judas, for I've betrayed others in my life;
and Peter, well—I've denied the Savior more than three times.

Drunk on the sweet nectar of the world only to find soberness in the power of His blood.
For I'm guilty of every sin—Oh wretched man I am!
Tomorrow I'll sin again—Oh wretched man I am!
Yet He still calls me friend, despite that I am.

Hold on, gotta gather myself:
What kind of love is this that one accepts me as I am?
Why would He call me friend, when I've rejected His hand?
Why would He call me friend, when I don't reverence his name?
There's no doubt my soul should be damned,
Yet I'm not because of this love I just don't understand.

So, I find myself in similar situations; doing the same old things over and over again.
I thought there would be a transformation since I accepted him as my Savior and King.
Did I fully understand what I was doing when I accepted His way of living?
Did I truly understand what I would forfeit to become in Him, a brand-new creature?

Truth is, I did, but tried to ignore what it would cost.
I want to be like Him, but without bearing my cross.
It's like my-cake-and-eat-it-too mentality;
I'll live however I choose for now, and when He returns,
I'll change so I can live with Him for eternity.

I'm a cup half full or maybe half empty,
but should that matter more than what's inside of it.
More concerned about my beginning, while not understanding,
that my ending will start a new beginning.

Like a leaf in the wind trying to withstand the currents of the world.
Foolish man hasn't figured out that his strength never was, and never will be enough.
For only one has overcome all temptation and has the power to throw the stone.
It is He who denied himself in the garden to be obedient unto God and continue on.
You know: Not my will but Your will be done!
No one ever told me it wouldn't be easy;
No one ever told me how an enemy could present himself as a friend to me
by closing my eyes to the One who died for me.
Is it worse to be blind in the eyes or in the mind?
Being able to see where you're going,
but not understand it's leading you to the fire.

I want to live right but according to Him;
Have the scales cleaned from my eyes so my vision is not skewed.
A complete renovation of my body, mind, and soul;
Built and maintained by the Spirit from above.
Strength provided to bear my cross,
And the wisdom to allow only Him to pour into my cup.

Finally:
To have a relationship of the greatest intimacy;
to share in a love that was first given unto me.
Then to understand that I am complete and made whole,
not because I'm perfect, but because of the holes.
The ones in his hands, feet, and side;
and the blood that was spilled that gives me life.

I will no longer condemn myself, or be guided and live according to my flesh.
I'm relinquishing my own authority to speak on my behalf,
for it's now clear to me that I don't know what's for my best.
Therefore, I simply let go, I just let go of it all,
and fall limp into His Holy hands;
So, He can show me my purpose and reveal to me the blueprint;
You know, of *The Plan*.

INTRODUCTION to "It Won't Fall"

Let's be honest. Marriage is not easy, and many have failed for various reasons. We believe that marriage is a step in one's life, instead of understanding that marriage itself is a life. When you make a vow before God, you have sworn an oath of commitment to an individual 'til death do you part. That sounds so easy to say, but it's difficult for many to fulfill. It begins with the definition of what love is and how it leads to marriage. Love has so many definitions, if you're talking about the world's definition; however, the love of God is clear and precise. It is God, and it endures all. It is not based on one's looks, their money, how good the sex is, or material things. Oftentimes, these are things that lead people to feel they are in love, but once these things start to fade or disappear, so does the love. Marriage is treated the same way. Very seldom do two people get married with a clear understanding that it's not theirs, but belongs to God, and anything of God is not temporary but eternal. Satan is always going to attack the things of God, and if the marriage is not built on the word of God, it will fail. It's a tragedy when we know this but still choose to believe we know better. Marriage is a beautiful and wonderful life for two to enjoy. It can last forever if it's guided, nurtured, and protected by God. For this to happen, we have to allow its foundation to be built on the word of God and not of the world. If you can turn it over to Him who cannot fail, then I can promise you "It Won't Fall"!

Supporting Scriptures

Genesis 2:24 — Therefore a man shall leave his father and his mother and hold fast to his wife, and they shall become one flesh.

Proverbs 18:22 — He who finds a wife finds a good thing and obtains favor from the Lord.

Jeremiah 17:7–8 — 7 "Blessed is the man who trusts in the Lord, whose trust is the Lord. 8 He is like a tree planted by water, that sends out its roots by the stream, and does not fear when heat comes, for its leaves remain green, and is not anxious in the year of drought, for it does not cease to bear fruit."

Hebrews 13:4 — Let marriage be held in honor among all, and let the marriage bed be undefiled, for God will judge the sexually immoral and adulterous.

1 Corinthians 3:10–14 — 10 According to the grace of God given to me, like a skilled master builder I laid a foundation, and someone else is building upon it. Let each one take care how he builds upon it. 11 For no one can lay a foundation other than that which is laid, which is Jesus Christ. 12 Now if anyone builds on the foundation with gold, silver, precious stones, wood, hay, straw. 13 each one's work will become manifest, for the Day will disclose it, because it will be revealed by fire, and the fire will test what sort of work each one has done. 14 If the work that anyone has built on the foundation survives, he will receive a reward.

1 Corinthians 13:4–7 — Love is patient and kind; love does not envy or boast; it is not arrogant or rude. It does not insist on its own way; it is not irritable or resentful; it does not rejoice at wrongdoing, but rejoices with the truth. Love bears all things, believes all things, hopes all things, endures all things.

IT WON'T FALL

My tears have deserted me for being used and abused.
Leaving late in the night like a black family moving;
no warning, just a note that said, "We up outta here!"
I thought about crying, but don't wanna resemble a drunk calling Earl,
only to find out that "Mr. Dry Heave" is the only one available.

This isn't supposed to be like this.
At least that's what I was taught to believe.
I guess ones understanding of love doesn't truly define love,
for true love can only be defined by the Divine.
I'm holding on for dear life, hoping love can find a way to cleanse itself
and meet me tomorrow looking like "Brand New Money."
If not, you'll see me on the corner asking if you can give a brother some change.

It's no longer a mystery to me why loving someone comes with a little pain.
No worries—I'm a grown man!
Yet my mind is that of an adolescent in trying to understand
how you can be with someone for years but truly only know their name.
That beauty and sex can cause you to be blind,
And make you believe it's about the gifts, trips, and don't forget the bump
and grind!

Changing lanes like an idiot driving a car can be the winds that steer the
course of a marriage.
If not careful, it can be blown in all directions,
but hold on with faith, 'cause there's One who is steady and stable.
I'm caught in the crosshairs of the world, knowing I'm surely to die but refuse to move.
Knowing I can be set free by the blood shed on the cross,

and surely live, but still to Thee, I refuse to go unto.
Still trying to hold on to something I think is forever,
when forever has never been a something, but Someone.
See, marriage is a commitment and vow between two: Man and Woman and God.
My bad, addition was not my strong suit, but three can equal two.

CHECK IT
Man and Wife are One and God makes two, which simply means,
don't try to make sense of Godly things by worldly things.
Even an ice cube can survive in hell if it be for only a second,
but marriage can survive hell forever if it's covered and protected.
Ya'll do remember Meshach, Shadrach, and Abednego.

PAY ATTENTION
Build your marriage on the world, and the world is its foundation
Standing strong and tall today, but sure to "pass away!"

QUESTIONS?
Who was your builder and decided your plans?
Did he have knowledge of issues that may arise and what will be required?
Did he give you a ten-year warranty, and with that you were satisfied?
Did he tell you that this foundation would stand and endure every storm?
Promise you that it would be still standing until the Savior returns?

The devil is a liar!
"I promise to tell the truth, the whole truth, and nothing but the truth."
Build a marriage upon the word of God, watch it stand firm and strong, and never fall.
Like the ice cube that only lasted a second;
cover it with the Blood of Jesus,
and from the fire, it's forever protected.
Take the worst of your spouse, place it in His hands,
receive the transformation tailored according to His plans.

Relinquishing your judgment and your fears;
accepting what is according to His will.
Then acknowledging the marriage is not yours,
but of Him that is all pure with everlasting love.
That unconditional love which is able to endure and overcome;
accepting your spouse's weaknesses and shortcomings.
A love that is not subject to the judgment of the world,
but is defined by its strength to overcome that of the world.
For God is first in all things; perfect in all His ways;
and never to share His honor and glory.
It is this love that gives me assurance
that marriage can withstand the stormy weather.
It is this love that fills me with joy,
'cause I know what He joins together is forever.

INTRODUCTION to "The One"

Who has the answer to life in its totality? Who understands fully why we can be godly at the break of dawn, and before the setting of the sun, ungodliness has resurfaced and taken control? What we struggle with is not so difficult to understand if we were to have a greater understanding of our Lord and Savior and the tricks of the enemy. For the majority, it's misinformation and a lack or desire to know, because life, according to the world, tells us this is okay and no big deal. However, this is a big deal! "The One" speaks about those who know Christ but struggle to live for Him or remain faithful. Being faithful does not mean being perfect, but instead means giving your life over to the Lord and, within the depths of your heart, truly believe and live according to His word, will, and way. Belief, then, is revealed in our living and heartfelt desire to please Him and hold close to our hearts his commands and statutes. There are struggles we will face, but never alone. There will be trials and tribulations, but never too much to bear. There will be days when you feel all alone, but He will never leave nor forsake, and days when you just want to give up and go back to the way things were, but that is a choice that can or will determine the eternal home of your soul. God has, is, and always will be more than enough. This world may paint a beautiful portrait that to some is a Picasso, but the paint on it is not authentic and will wash away. The canvas God uses is one of a kind, and the paint can't be erased or removed. The finished product is priceless and can only be housed in one place, and that's the Kingdom of Heaven. Ladies and gentleman, with all you may go through, know nothing you endure or be offered can ever be more comforting or fulfilling than "The One"!

List Your Supporting Scriptures:

THE ONE

I see many paths, but none are right for me.
Eyes watering from attempting to focus on where this life is taking me.
Puzzled by unspeakable thoughts,
yet could these thoughts be the missing piece of the puzzle?

Glass windows shattered by words unspoken;
misleading affection that's confused with love and devotion.
Gotta sit my tail down and rest awhile,
'cause running this race has taken its toll;
truth be spoken, I'm mentally and emotionally broken.

I can feel the good in me leaking out, and slowly but surely,
I fear that old man is lurking about.
Trying to reclaim territory taken.
Hoping that the landlord is unaware or not concerned with my situation.

Fed up but not full; hot as fish grease but still cool.
Wanna run but choose to stroll; I choose God instead of riches and gold.
Lord, guide me and grant me peace in my soul!

Fragmented imagination, can't get a clear picture.
Stagnant dedication to this life God has given.
Like loose-leaf paper without a binder;
no grooves to secure my heart, my soul, or my mind.

Thoughts all over the place like kids on a playground.
Be careful, for the word says an idle mind is where the evil one can be found.

Now my tank on low but refuse to stop for gas.
Flesh weak, still foolish enough to put it to the test.
No bars to hold me; no potter to mold me;
and no carpenter to salvage me;
sometimes feeling the wrong that I've done
disqualifies me from His forgiveness.

Oh man with no faith or vision to see, that the blood is more than enough
for me.
Can I tell you a secret?
A life without God is a life not worth living.

I hope tomorrow includes me,
but on this night I'm gonna fall down on my knees.
For the cross is very heavy;
wish I could let it go, but God won't let me.

This is my struggle but not mines alone.
This is my calling in which I'ma own.
No part-time servants needed;
those who show up on Sunday giving praise,
and then serve the world the rest of the week.
They're like paper plates-used for soup,
not equipped to hold or contain the word of truth.

I remember this life when I was blind;
recall the day the scales were removed from my eyes.
Now gotta stay focused; don't want to deal with the locust;
and though I live in this world, don't have to be of it.

Now I'll die to my will for your will, so that one day I can live
in that place just beyond the river.
Oh, and how joyful it will be when I'm finally free.

Living with my Father for all eternity.
Even though I can't see it, by faith I believe it;
even though I can't see Him, His spirit flows, and I can feel it.
And if He never blesses me again, still I'll praise Him.
For He is God and God alone, you know, The One!

INTRODUCTION to "Wake Up"

There is more required of Christians than praying, going to church, and Bible study. Understanding the example, Christ himself, who prayed, visited, and taught in the synagogues. However, there were so many other very important aspects and responsibilities He left for us to emulate. None can be totally like Him because He is perfect in all His ways and one without sin. The body of Christ is suffering to lead those who are lost to the God who can heal and save simply because they no longer understand they are servants and servants serve. Their mentality is that there has to be something in it for them to help another. They also have an unwillingness to give up one's self to bless or build up another; and the inability to reflect the light of godliness to those whom lamps have no oil. Jesus came to serve and give up His life for a people that were undeserving of an ounce of His blood. Unselfish by giving up His will for His Father's while knowing that the world would continue to reject Him over and over again. "Wake Up" speaks to those who are Christians but refuse to give of themselves to advance the Kingdom of Heaven. Their hands are forever out, asking God for something but never asking God what they can do for Him or another. This contradicts the behavior of Christ and is causing those who are lost to no longer look for the light in those who have tasted God's goodness, grace, and mercy. It has never been and never will be about us, but instead, that which God has called us to be. Ladies and gentleman, it's time for us to "Wake Up"!

WAKE UP

Tears unborn because of one's pride and lack of compassion.
Hand like Chik-fil-a, closed on Sunday,
but always lifted up to God wanting something.
You look the part, but not qualified; given the role, but not justified.
Now acting out the scene, but not glorified.
Your life wasted because none of this did God decide.

Living your best life—it's all good,
but what about the next life when God gets to choose.
Oh, now I got ya thinking but your flesh still got you drinking
that same old Kool-Aid; you know the flavor—Hell!
Don't want to be harsh but the sword cuts both ways.
You can try to shut my mouth, but the rocks will still cry out and praise.

Has it ever occurred to you He might come back today?
Where you at? What you doing?
If you blink your eyes, you may no longer see the one standing next to you.
Let me Selah before I shout a hallelujah;
'cause when that fire jumps upon you, it takes control and won't let go of ya.

Okay, where was I…
I see one who claims to be in the heavenly army of God.
Armor on but afraid of a dart;
and refuse to share their seat on the bus to God's house.
Quick to pronounce one dead instead of trying to resuscitate;
can't serve anyone else but always waiting for their plate.
Sitting at the master's table all dignified and entitled;
if one didn't know any better, they'd think you're one of the original disciples.
Be careful, for everyone here is not who they claim to be.

For my Lord did say:
"The one who dips his bread in the dish with me will also betray me."

Now your words need detergent.
You're supposed to be an ally, but you're the insurgent.
But I gotcha right where I want ya.
So full of yourself that you've outgrown your britches.
Been cut and torn by the world, and don't realize you need heavenly stitches.
All holy but only unto yourself,
quoting scripture with the best of them,
Yet, it's not reflected in your steps.

Your eyes wide open but you will fail to see the power of the one that goes
before me.
The transformation of what I used to be because of what's inside of me.
So, I come to you face to face; not to cause you harm but to open my arms.
And remind you that those who see and encounter you,
Should also see and encounter the son. Wake up!

INTRODUCTION to "All Good"

The word of God states in Matthew 6:21, "Wherever your treasure is, there your heart will be also." What we've learned in life is the things we are sensitive to are those that are personal or have had a negative or positive affect on those closest to us. In a world full of darkness and filled with various temptations that gnaw and tug at the desires within us, causing instability in who we are, how we live, and mostly, what we submit to, there is a strong belief of determining what is or isn't good. We use the term for many things based on our cognizant reasoning, upbringing, current environment, and, sadly, what the world has concluded. "All Good" shines a very bright light on how Christian behavior is fragile and unstable when it should be built on a firm foundation that can't be moved. This behavior is a result of how we continue to have a relationship with the flesh and things of the world which entice us through our natural senses. God is patient, understanding, forgiving, loving, and full of grace and mercy when it comes to His dealings with our shortcomings. His ways are not our ways, thoughts are not our thoughts; therefore, know this, God and God alone is the only one who can determine what is good, because He is the only one that is "All Good." We present to you "All Good"!

List Your Supporting Scriptures:

ALL GOOD

Self-indulgence of myself; I've now succumbed to the power of the flesh.
It appears to have given me some authority, such as cleaning, feeding, and
covering it.
Yet I keep hearing this gentle whisper speaking within me,
that this authority given will lead to a spiritual death sentence.

You see, power, money, and adversity are intangibles that can peel back the skin.
Allowing one's true self to be revealed;
And that which is hidden to no longer be hid.
But to the man that is blind, this is meaningless.
Even though he sees it with his own eyes, still he refuses to believe it.
What's worse?
A man with no legs or arms with a heart that loves God,
or a man with riches but doesn't know the love of God.

Ponder that for a moment……
Ice cycles of gold, fancy cars, and fine clothes represent the branches hang-
ing from my tree.
While to my right, I see souls once lost with treasures that cannot be bought,
washed in the blood and attached by love; to one whose roots are heavenly,
and branches are unbreakable and healthy.
Kinda wondering what must I do to be connected to that tree?

Keep pondering and I'll get back to ya….
If I tell you I love you, how would you know it?
Is it because I speak to your attractiveness, which should only be a fraction
of what love truly is.
Or do my reactions toward your ugliness become the denominator that confirms
my every thought, action, or situation, and determines what my love is or isn't.

Or even worse, based on who's in my ear or present.

Wilted flowers that can't grow in soil that's good
speaks to the inappropriate seeds that you willingly received,
and allowed to be planted in your vineyard.
Don't worry, you can't plant an apple seed and expect oranges;
and you can't plant the unholy in the holy and expect to reap a harvest.

Gotta tidbit for ya…
One brother's territory is based on location, while the others' is according to
the creator.

Lend me your ear….
What good is a love that is defined by things?
Transparent to the eye and stimulate my senses, but unaware of what's beneath.
God's love is built only on love,
maybe because God is love, and can be nothing less, but so much more.
The infinity of the Alpha and Omega;
the remembrance of the cross and lamb that bled and died to save us
Can separate the glitter from the gold so you can clearly see,
those who are the sheep and those who are the goats.

Understand the purpose of love according to the world,
so you enjoy it, and continuously indulge.
The truth is, worldly love is based on things,
but true love is pure and everlasting, given by the great I Am.

So, make your choice, be willing to live with it.
For when it's over and done, the love you choose to rest within you
will be the same that may or may not love you,
for better or worse, richer or poorer, in sickness and health…

My bad!

Got caught up in the now when I meant to be speaking of what will be as He returns on a cloud.

Simply put:
The one you choose to love and allow to love you will be the same one you'll spend an eternity with.
And know this: Love is only good when it's from He that was, is, and forever will be "All Good."

INTRODUCTION to "The Things He Do"

We deserve nothing, and God owes us nothing except that which is in His word. God has the authority to do for one and not for another, and even in these actions, He still is God and nothing less. Abundantly, He blesses us with spiritual gifts. Some the gift of prophesy, while others the gift of teaching, preaching, laying of the hands, or prayer. The constant here is that God distributes these seeds for servitude, which are sometimes accompanied by other blessings that are "just because" you belong to Me, and I'm your God. This is where God's children lose focus and no longer retain a clear picture of who He is, regardless of whether they've tasted his sweetness and received prior blessings. What is it that God owes any of us? What have we done to have our hands out with a sense of entitlement based on what we feel should be given us, or what another has been given that should be ours. The Bible teaches us to rejoice when another is blessed. Not to compare what God is doing in their lives to what He's doing in ours. God is sovereign in all His ways, perfect and infallible, and blesses according to His wisdom of what one requires to fulfill His purpose in them. There is a tendency to judge God based on what He has or has not done which causes many to lose their way. God is God alone, and doesn't require our finite wisdom to determine how, who, and when He should bless someone. For when He blesses, it will always be to prosper and not harm and draw you closer to Him. Ladies and gentlemen, we present to you "The Things He Do"!

List Your Supporting Scriptures:

THE THINGS HE DO

Have you ever heard the footsteps of an angel?
Or embraced its beauty when its wings are folded.
Been taken up to view the wonders of the second heaven,
and be in the company of Job, Daniel, and Paul, God's chosen.

Have you felt his presence that causes time to stand still?
Or be awakened for a midnight rendezvous in which you were not informed.
Felt the belt from above when you step out of his will,
then understand there are times God desires you and you alone.

Images of faces that seem harmless to the eye;
spiritual discernment that radiates and melts the disguise.
Gifts not deserved and grace unworthy;
still showering down simply because my Father loves me

In my thoughts now….
Why do the rich struggle with finances?
And criminals squander away second and third chances.
I was given a mule but not the forty acres.
Didn't ask the giver the reason why, so I chose to ride it because I'm lazy.
Now we're both broke down and tired.

Gotta leave that alone….

A developed mind is one with comprehension;
Fluid in understanding things studied.
Yet God can place something much greater within you
that was promised after He who rose that was once buried.
Gifts that can't be wrapped in paper;

a fire that can't be extinguished.
Visions manifested that appear and become vapor;
hope and love once lost, now fully replenished.
A power unimaginable and healing indescribable;
yet one's doubt still has the strength to remain.
So he parted a sea, drew water from a rock;
then opened a ground for Korah and those on his block
Who chose not to recognize and reverence His name.

Now ya saying something!

So find a penny and pick it up, and all the day you'll have good luck.
Or find a penny and lift it up, ask God to bless it, believe and trust,
that something so simple will become amazingly extravagant.
Because God does exceedingly and abundantly above anything you could ask for.

Okay, what about this?
I have not because I ask not, Yet I've asked and do not have.
Do the math—okay!
So he learned obedience through suffering, yet never sinned.
In our suffering, we become more disobedient,
because we refuse to surrender unto Him.
Do I need to say that again?
Naw, I'ma leave it alone 'cause you either get it or don't.
You know, all The Things He Do.

INTRODUCTION to "The Ugly Truth"

Many saints will not admit there are times they've questioned God's presence during a time of need. They will not admit that living as a Christian sometimes requires strength to take the high road when everyone else is taking the low; assist someone that has mistreated and slandered your name; bless someone that refused to help you in your time of need; and maintain holiness and righteousness in a world full of darkness. Living a life for Christ is not easy, but remember, it wasn't easy for Christ to live a life for God and fulfill the purpose in which He was sent. As a Christian, you will go through periods where life presents you with so many trials and tribulations and offers you a way out. The flesh man will view these events and quickly recommend that you just go back to where and who you once were; whereas, the Spirit of God will hold you still as it deals with the toils of life and restores your faith that God will always fight your battles, and never leave or forsake you. When you come to this point in your walk, it is okay to go to the Father and be transparent about how you're feeling, for He cares about all our problems. He is a God of compassion, understanding, patience, and love. Furthermore, He is all-knowing, which means He already knows. "The Ugly Truth" speaks of one that is standing before the Almighty and being transparent, while maintaining a humble and reverent approach to the throne of grace. Ladies and gentlemen, I present to you "The Ugly Truth"!

List Your Supporting Scriptures:

THE UGLY TRUTH

I've cried out to God many times.
Got angry, felt he didn't answer.
Led to thoughts of why should I keep believing
that I would never be left or forsaken.
I've pondered going back; being un-reborn,
for it feels like I'm no better now before being transformed.

I've walked the straight and narrow.
Thought a few friends would be on this path.
And with so many obstacles to overcome,
that I've began to look for an exit,
you know—the greener grass!
For sometimes I feel I'm walking alone,
And that you've allowed upon me, so much pain and suffering.
Question: Am I truly one of the ones you call your own?

In my spirit I feel conflicted,
because the flesh feels so good, but restricted.
In my temptations, I move without hesitation,
only to find myself at the edge of the cliff and offered my every desire,
in exchange for my soul's salvation.

Sometimes I feel like I'm headed toward heaven,
but all I see around me is the desert.
You say I'm a king's child, but truthfully speaking,
I feel like a village peasant.
Am I like the children of Israel?
Love you but when trouble comes,
wanna go back to where you've brought me from.

Or am I like Judas?
Chosen by you and loved by you,
yet still willing to betray you for something of the world
I believe is better and greater than you.

This is the ugly truth that I'm speaking to you.
Not because I'm rebellious,
But because I still trust and believe in you.
This is the ugly truth that I'm speaking to you,
and I pray and hope that you hear me,
so that you would remind me you're still here with me,
and I still belong to you.
This, my Father, is my Ugly Truth.

INTRODUCTION to "Black Woman, Please!"

Her worth is greater than the most precious jewel you can find. Her beauty is sweet and gentle, yet at the same time, intimidating. However, that beauty and worth are sometimes lost in the way she presents herself. The way she dresses and speaks; the attention she desires; but mostly, her misunderstanding of strength that is truly low self-esteem. Her eyes that should guide her, and mind that should discern, have been distorted by worldly values and standards. This results in her lack of understanding of what a strong black man is and his worth. Yet at the end of the day, the divine and godly beauty of the black woman has for thousands of years been a desire not for only her black king but also others. It is critical that she comes to understand who and what she represents. It is even more important that she comes to understand the power in which she possesses. Ladies and gentlemen, we hope you enjoy and understand why I'm crying out "Black Woman, Please!"

Supporting Scriptures

Genesis 2:21–23 — 21 So the Lord God caused a deep sleep to fall upon the man, and while he slept took one of his ribs and closed up its place with flesh. 22 And the rib that the Lord God had taken from the man he made into a woman and brought her to the man. 23 Then the man said,
"This at last is bone of my bones, and flesh of my flesh; she shall be called Woman, because she was taken out of Man."

Proverbs 14:1 — The wisest of women builds her house, but folly with her own hands tears it down.

Psalms 139:13–14 — 13 For you formed my inward parts; you knitted me together in my mother's womb. 14 I praise you, for I am fearfully and wonderfully made; Wonderful are your works; my soul knows it very well.

1 Peter 3:1–6 — 1 Likewise, wives, be subject to your own husbands, so that even if some do not obey the word, they may be won without a word by the conduct of their wives, 2 when they see your respectful and pure conduct. 3 Do not let your adorning be external—the braiding of hair and the putting on of gold jewelry, or the clothing you wear— 4 but let your adorning be the hidden person of the heart with the imperishable beauty of a gentle and quiet spirit, which in God's sight is very precious. 5 For this is how the holy women who hoped in God used to adorn themselves, by submitting to their own husbands, 6 as Sarah obeyed Abraham, calling him lord. And you are her children, if you do good and do not fear anything that is frightening.

Titus 2:3–5 — 3 Older women likewise are to be reverent in behavior, not slanderers or slaves to much wine. They are to teach what is good, 4 and so train the young women to love their husbands and children, 5 to be self-controlled, pure, working at home, kind, and submissive to their own husbands, that the word of God may not be reviled.

BLACK WOMAN, PLEASE!

Black Woman, please!
Shut your mouth.
'Cause those that came before you have already spoken for you.
Still your tongue cuts like the whips on their backs.
Tearing away at the fabric of your strong black man.
Be careful;
for that very fabric may be what you need for cover and protection.

Oh, I know you're fine and beautifully designed;
the Creator put in His best work.
Yet, what He intended for all to see is lost in your insecurities.
Yeah—you know, I'm talking about them insecurities;
the ones that are showing like naps on the back of your neck.
Though you think they're hidden by the five-hundred-dollar lace wig you wear;
trust this: even weeds peek out of cracks in concrete.

Black Woman, please!
Sit your ass down.
Be seen and not heard, but be heard by what they see.
Your round hips and full lips represent your ancestors from across the way.
And though you didn't suffer the ride across,
the world reminds you that the boat named *Racism* still drifts along the shore.
Intimidated by what they once hated, curious about how sweet it would be
to taste ya.
You know that "Ooo Wee" or that "Good Thang."
'Cause a black woman is a black woman when she's fully dressed,
and not showing you a damn thang.

Black Woman, please!

Take your rightful place and don't move.
For the stability of your man's foundation is in the rib that God took to
make ya.
Understand you're the weaker vessel,
yet unto God you're not less than the man that He created for you.
Just remember: no talking to snakes and don't bite them apples;
run away if you have to—Black Woman, please, RUN.

Black Woman, please!
Respect the sensitivity of your black man with understanding.
For his tears don't make him weak,
but allow him to express himself without words that cut deep, or hands that
beat.
What you say, Black Woman? You want a thug in your life.
Saggy pants, nappy 'fro, and quick to step to a brotha, but slow to find a job.
Using your money to spend on his other honey while you're working your
black ass off.
Black Woman, please!

Black Woman, please!
Open your eyes.
For you are what the world despises.
You are what the world refuses to recognize.
You are what the world wants to minimize.
They close their eyes, but I know they feel it
That fire from your grace and beauty
they don't have the power to quench—You dig!

But Black Woman, please:
Get it together and stay right where you are.
'Cause a queen only answers to her king.
See, money can never equal your worth.
And though the man is the head,

he can never give what you give—new birth.
So, thrive in your place and your purpose.
You're Proverbs 31, I call you virtuous.
You're the mother of the house, I call you the nurturer.
And for those that paved the way and came before ya,
Let them know their labor has not been in vain
And that your life will honor them.
But make sure your life first honors Him—The Father
—Black Woman, please!

SOMETHING I WANTED TO SHARE TOO
BY ROOSEVELT FRANKLIN

First and foremost, I want to thank my God, the only true and living God, who has blessed me abundantly. The greatest joy I have in my life is that I'm a servant of God, and He calls me his friend. I would also be remised if I didn't thank my grandfather and grandmother, who raised me and taught me Christian values and morals that still today guide me in many aspects of my life. My grandmother, Elizabeth Harris, was my first experience in the presence of an angel of God. Her wisdom and guidance through some of the toughest times in my life reminded me God will always provide what you need and never forsake you. I also want to thank the woman that keeps it tight and 100, my beautiful wife Miesha, for encouraging me to trust in God during the times I struggled to understand his plan for me. She is my rib, and I give all glory, honor, and thanks to God for the blessing of spending my life with her.

In the midst of all God has blessed me with, there are four children I'm honored to be the father of. I've always known and yet didn't always understand the beauty of the gift God gives to us when he blesses us with children. They teach us how to be loving and patient; how to navigate through their individualities while at the same time, keeping the knowledge of the God we serve fresh in their hearts and minds. It is our responsibility and one I've always welcomed and treasured.

The mighty word of God is the only foundation in which I try to live my life as a husband, father, brother, friend, and member of the body of Christ. Throughout my life, I've strayed at times in my life and followed the world; for that I am not proud. Because His calling and gifts are irrevocable, I've always heard His voice call for to come back to Him, back under the umbrella of His covering. His mercy and love cannot be fathomed; by sending His only begotten Son He shows me just how much He loves me. I owe God everything because there is no doubt in my mind, I would be still lost in the wilderness had not He led me to his Son. I've done nothing deserving of this love, but "It surely feels good!"

As we started to prepare this book, we found ourselves questioning whether or not we were worthy to say some of the things that are written. In the end, God reminded us that it is not for us to question whether we are worthy or able, but instead, to trust and be obedient to whatever God instructs us to say. He is the one who validates, justifies, and qualifies. There are so many ways to live that are not captured in these writings; however, we did our best to remove ourselves from the process and only write what God was pouring into us. Some of these writings are very personal, while others are experienced based. There are also writings about Christians and how I've witnessed our behavior; how we carry ourselves in the eyes of the world, but mostly how we carry ourselves in the eyes of God. In everything we do, we should do to please the Father. In our own capacity we fall short, but our efforts should never fall short. Let's encourage one another each and every day; speaking life not death, even unto those who have wronged us. Let's show the world who God is through our actions; we are set apart. We can never believe that we are any better than the ones lost and trying to find their way out of the wilderness. We have to shine our lights to showcase our Father in an inviting way so those in darkness will want to come to the light to be received by Christ.

Lastly, I want to thank everyone who took the time to read these poems. I pray you're all blessed in ways unimaginable, and that whatever God has in store you'll be positioned to receive. We are at war with the enemy; therefore, he wants to tear our marriages apart, kill our dreams, convince us God is not for us and that "The Blood" cannot save us. Please, let's take the fight to the enemy and fight together to defeat him. Put on the full armor of God daily, knowing that we have power and dominion over him through Christ Jesus; the victory is already ours. Please continue to pray for me as I press on in the fight. I will not grow weary in well doing but will continue to hoist my flag which reads, "He is the risen Christ, and he is coming back for Me!" May God bless and keep you all. I Love all of you with the love of Christ and share in the wonderful opportunity to have been chosen to be placed in His hands. In God's hands, no man can ever pluck us out. Oh mighty God, such a beautiful love, such a beautiful love!

Roosevelt Franklin

We pray that you've been inspired to jot down your own testimony. If you have, please use the blank pages provided below to begin your journey. Who knows, it may be something you, too, one day will decide to share.

ABOUT THE AUTHORS

Roosevelt and Miesha Franklin professed their love before God on March 15, 2002. They are a blended family comprised of four children and two grandchildren. They share a passion for witnessing to couples and inspiring healthy marriages.

In their free time, the duo enjoys writing music and poetry, cooking, sporting events, lawn and gardening, and the exploration of the arts. Over the past 21 years they have experienced the beauty of God's love within their marriage, even during times of adversity.

Through this work, they aspire to encourage the Body of Christ to remain steadfast.